Y0-BLS-424

Caring for Our ANIMALS

Carol Greene

ENSLOW PUBLISHERS, INC.
Bloy St. & Ramsey Ave.   P.O. Box 38
Box 777   Aldershot
Hillside, N.J. 07205   Hants GU12 6BP
U.S.A.

Copyright © 1991 by Enslow Publishers, Inc.

All rights reserved.

No part of this book may be reproduced by any means without the written permission of the publisher.

Library of Congress Cataloging-in-Publication Data

Greene, Carol.
    Caring for our animals / Carol Greene.
       p. cm.—(Caring for our earth)
    Includes index.
    Summary: Simple text and illustrations describe issues related to animals, such as habitat destruction, pet care, the fur trade, etc., and activities children can do to protect animals.
    ISBN 0-89490-352-7
    1. Animals—Juvenile literature. 2. Wildlife conservation—Juvenile literature. [1. Animals. 2. Wildlife conservation.] I. Title. II. Series: Greene, Carol. Caring for our earth.
QL49.G75 1991   91-9237
333.95′4—dc20   CIP
                                                                  AC

Printed in the United States of America

10 9 8 7 6 5 4 3 2 1

Photo Credits: Margaret Cooper, pp. 4, 6, 10, 13, 15, 17, 18, 24; Humane Society of Missouri/Laura Cook, pp. 23, 27; R. Roger Pryor, pp. 7, 20; Quinta Scott, pp. 12, 21; United States Department of Agriculture, p. 9.

Cover Photo: Margaret Cooper

Contents

What Is It? 5

Why Are Animals Important? 8

What Can Happen to Animals? . . 16

What Can We Do? 25

What Can You Do? 28

Words to Know 30

Index 31

About the Author 32

Elephants are large animals.

What Is It?

It is large or small
or middle-sized.
It is wild or tame.
It is alive and beautiful.
What is it? An animal.

Elephants, whales,
and ladybugs are animals.
So are birds, fish, frogs,
turtles, and spiders.

Ants are very small animals. But there are many of them. Some live in huge hills like this.

People have named about 750,000 kinds of insects and thousands of other kinds of animals.

But there are still many more that we don't know about.

Each kind of animal has a place on the earth. Each does something. Each is important.

This bullfrog is a small animal.

Why Are Animals Important?

Animals are important
because they help nature.

Bees carry pollen
from flower to flower.
Then the flowers make seeds,
and new plants grow.

Birds carry seeds
from place to place
and help new plants grow.

This bee has pollen stuck to her. She will leave some of it on another flower.

This squirrel
has found one
nut he buried.
But he won't
find all of them.

Squirrels bury many nuts to eat later. Sometimes, they can't find all of them. From these lost nuts, new trees grow.

Animals help the soil.

When they die, their
bodies become part of it.
Worms dig tunnels in soil
and help it get air.

Animals help people, too.
We get food from
some of them.

From cows we get
milk, butter, and cheese.
From hens we get eggs,
and from bees we get honey.
People also eat the meat
of many kinds of animals.

We get clothes
from animals too.

We use wool from sheep
and leather from cattle.
We use silk from silkworms.

Many years ago, people
wore furry animal skins
to keep warm.
Some people still do.
Others say we don't need
to wear furs anymore.

People wear clothes made from the wool of sheep.

Cats help people by catching mice.

Animals help people
by getting rid of pests.
Cats catch mice.
Ladybugs and other insects
eat pests that harm crops.
So do birds and bats.

People ride animals such as
horses, donkeys, and camels.
Sometimes these animals
pull or carry things, too.

Some animals help
in special ways.
Dogs lead blind people
or sniff out hidden drugs.

Animals also help people
by being their friends.
People keep many kinds
of animals as pets.

Animals are important because
they help in many ways.
But most of all,
they are important
just because they are.

Each animal is alive.
Each is beautiful.
The earth is home for each
and so each is important.

This girl and her dog have fun together.

What Can Happen to Animals?

Many people don't care about animals. They are the worst enemy that animals have.

Wild animals lose their homes and even their lives because of some people.

People cut down the forests
where some animals live.
They drain the water
from wetlands where
others make their homes.

People put all kinds of things
into rivers, lakes, and oceans.

People in China are
trying to save places
for pandas to live.

It is the governments' job
to take care of the refuges
and keep the animals safe.

But sometimes governments
let hunters kill the animals.
They let people cut down trees
and dig mines in refuges.
Then the animals are not safe.

An animal such as this opossum can get sick or hurt from litter on the land.

People harm tame animals, too.
Some farmers crowd
their animals together
in dark, smelly places.

They tie them so that
they cannot move around.

It isn't good for pigs to be crowded like this.

They take baby animals
away from their mothers.

Other people don't take
good care of their pets.
They forget to give them
food and fresh water.
They leave them outside
in the rain and cold.

Some don't take
their pets to the vet.
They never play with them.
They forget to love them.
People like this
should not have pets.

Pets need care and love, too.

This is a happy pet.

What Can We Do?

People need to remember
that the earth belongs
to animals, too.
People must take
better care of the earth.

They must stop cutting down
so many forests and
leave the wetlands alone.
They must stop spilling and
dumping things into the water.

People can keep the air clean.
They can stop littering.
They can tell governments
to take better care of
refuges for wild animals.

Farmers can be kinder
to their animals.
They can give them
better places to live.

People can take care of pets
and treat them as friends.
They can make more laws
to protect animals.
Many groups are working
to get such laws made.

You can find great pets at an animal shelter.

What Can You Do?

You can help animals.
Here are some things
that you can do.

1. Keep the earth clean.
   Pick up litter when you can.
   Don't let balloons get away.
   Cut six-pack holders apart
   or ask an adult to do it.
   You might save an animal!

2. Feed the birds all winter.
   Don't stop, because they
   will count on your food.
   Put out water for them in summer.

3. Don't squash harmless insects.
   Help them to a safe place.

4. Learn about your pet
   and what it needs.
   Choose pets from
   animal shelters.
   Shelters have great animals.

5. Sit still and watch
   an animal for a while.
   Then write a poem about it.

Words to Know

animal shelter—A place that cares for lost or unwanted animals.

pet—An animal that lives with people and is their good friend.

pollen—Part of a plant that often looks like dust.

pollutant (poh-LOOT-ent)—A thing left over after burning or making something. It is harmful to the earth.

refuge—A place where wild animals can be safe.

soil—A mix of ground-up rock, dead plants and animals, air, and water.

starve—To die from not having food.

vet—An animal doctor; short for veterinarian.

wetland—A place where the soil holds a lot of water.

Index

air, 11, 26
animals
    beauty of, 15
    crowding of, 21
    importance of, 6, 8-15
    kinds of, 5, 6
    safety of, 20, 28
    shelters for, 27, 29
    tame, 21
    uses of, 8-15
    wild, 16, 19, 26
balloons, 19, 28
bees, 8, 9, 11
birds, 8, 13, 29
China, 17
clothes, 11-12

earth, 6, 15, 25, 28
flowers, 8, 9
food, 11, 29
forests, 17, 25
    as home for animals, 17
fur, 12
government, 20, 26
insects, 6, 11, 13, 29
laws, 26
litter, 19, 28
nuts, 10
oil, 19
people, 6, 11, 13, 16, 17, 18
    as enemies to animals, 16-23
pests, 13

pets, 14, 23, 24, 26, 27, 29
   care of, 23, 26
plants, 8
pollen, 8, 9
pollutants, 19
refuges, 19-20, 26
   hunters on, 20
   mines in, 20
seeds, 8

seeing-eye dogs, 14
six-pack holders, 19, 28
soil, 10, 11
   tunnels in, 11
trash, 19
trees, 10, 20
water, 17, 25
wetlands, 17, 18, 25
   as home for animals, 17

About the Author

Carol Greene is the author of about 100 books for children. She has also worked as a children's editor and a teacher of writing for children. Ms. Greene shares her home with 3 cats and 3 dogs. When her writing and pets allow it, she enjoys gardening, music, and doing volunteer work at her church.